STEWARDSHIP

STEWARDSHIP
How To Steward Your Way Into A Steadfast Walk With God

Georgelyn Edwards-Wilkerson

XULON PRESS ELITE

Xulon Press Elite
2301 Lucien Way #415
Maitland, FL 32751
407.339.4217
www.xulonpress.com

© 2021 by Georgelyn Edwards-Wilkerson

All rights reserved solely by the author. The author guarantees all contents are original and do not infringe upon the legal rights of any other person or work. No part of this book may be reproduced in any form without the permission of the author. The views expressed in this book are not necessarily those of the publisher.

Unless otherwise indicated, Scripture quotations taken from the King James Version (KJV) – *public domain.*

Scripture quotations taken from the Amplified Bible (AMP). Copyright © 1954, 1958, 1962, 1964, 1965, 1987 by The Lockman Foundation. Used by permission. All rights reserved.

Paperback ISBN-13: 978-1-6628-0294-2
eBook ISBN-13: 978-1-6628-0295-9

Dedication

In remembrance of my parents: Elgin Edwards & Augustina Edwards

And to my siblings who stand with me today always reminding me of the values that were instilled in us by our parents who will never be forgotten.

Brothers: David Edwards
Jules Edwards
Winfield Edwards
Edwin Edwards
Isaac Edwards
Lyndon Edwards
Sisters: Midlane Edwards
Megan Edwards-Henry

Acknowledgements

First, I want to thank the Father, Son *and Holy Spirit who* inspired me to write this book to encourage and build up the body of Christ.

I must thank God for my Apostles Dorreth and Alpheus Todman. Specially, Apostle Dorreth Todman who by the Holy Spirit called me out and mentored me, praying me through into who I have become today. It is because of her giving me God's instructions, this book is in print today.

I want to thank my Shekinah Glory family, fellow laborers in the Lord. You are a family to me indeed. My source of encouragement and spiritual support. I love you all very much.

Special thanks to my Husband and prayer partner, my encourager on this path of righteousness Elijah B Wilkerson and my sons Elijah and Kenneth Wilkerson. I love you all dearly.

STEWARDSHIP

To my dear sister in the Lord, Etlyn Steele who took the time to pre-edit this book, thank you.

Special thank you to my sister-in-law Bessie Wilkerson who gave me the push to publish this book when I was at a standstill. God's blessings be upon you.

> *I found Stewardship to be a "thought-provoking" book as well as strengthening for my own spiritual journey. Its content is rich as it personifies God's calling and hand upon this Author's life. Personally, I have come to know the Author as a passionate, devoted Woman of God exemplifying a focused mindset for Kingdom business; day-in and day out. As she shares her godly-walk of faith, you will soon discover her love and mission for souls on the battlefield for Christ. I felt blessed to glean through these pages and wish her God's continued blessing(s). This is only the beginning...The Best is Yet to Come, in Jesus Name; Amen!*
>
> *Etlyn Steele*

Preface

Thank you for picking up this little book with huge potential! In the lives of most Christians we can all attest to the fact that occasionally we need someone to come along side us and whisper some helpful advice. In turn we have been both giver of words of wisdom and grateful recipients.

This book on stewardship lays a rich foundation on items of vital importance to those of us who desire to live the best total representation of Jesus and embody the virtues associated with a human life well lived. In this book we are admonished in love to consider how we can employ strategies to do just that.

The information is laid out in a plain, forthright manner with little room for misinterpretation. The author covers such important aspects of Christian character as physical, financial, spiritual health and wellbeing as she delves into the responsibility of all citizens of the kingdom to possess their vessels in sanctification and honor.

STEWARDSHIP

As the author's Husband, I can say both objectively and subjectively that she seeks every day to live the life she preaches about. Her advice is sound, and it has also encouraged my walk with the Lord as I go on to perfection. So, grab a comfortable chair, your spiritual magnifying glass and your prayerful mind as we look to our dear sister for her insights into stewardship.

Enjoy!

Pastor Elijah B. Wilkerson

Table of Contents

Stewardship 1

Spiritual 11

Physical 29

Mental 43

Social 53

Financial 67

Citations: 81

Stewardship

SUB: Stewarding Your Way
into a Steadfast Walk with God

I COME FROM A FAMILY OF ELEVEN: FATHER, mother, and nine children—six boys and three girls. When I was a very young child, I remember my dad first as a fisherman. One day, he went to sea and was delayed way beyond his usual time. I can remember my mother being concerned before we went to bed. She was very troubled and feared that she would lose her husband, leaving her with nine little children.

Upon my father's return, my mother expressed her fears and told him she did not want him to continue being a fisherman, although that was his only source of supporting the family. My father, being an ambitious man, decided to heed my mom's advice and turned his ambition and attention to farming. He grew cows, goats, sheep, and even chickens. He also grew ground provisions, plantains, and bananas for export.

STEWARDSHIP

Having a vision for his family, my father set out to purchase different parcels of land to support and separate his livestock and growing fields. With the intention that his children would inherit the land, even if they did not farm it, they would always have a place to build or use as they saw fit. In all my father's ambition and hard work, he always instilled in us the need for education, godly principles, honest dealings, and good work ethic.

Just as my dad was a good steward over the financial part, my mom's domain was the home. She shared and supported his vision by making sure that his children and home were kept in a way that would make him proud. In an effort to share the blessings they received, my mother never cooked a meal with only our household in mind. It was her daily practice to prepare meals for her parents while they were alive. She would also give to anyone in need, and because of this, God always provided her with more to give. It is this example that first introduced me to the biblical principle of good stewardship.

TEXT: Luke 16:1-4, 10-13 and Genesis 39-40

Stewardship:

An ethic that embodies the responsible planning and management of resources (Wikipedia).

Utilizing and managing all resources God provides to the glory of God and the betterment of His creation.

The conducting, supervising, or managing of something—the careful and responsible management of something entrusted in one's care.

This concept of stewardship should be applied in every area of our lives—spiritually, physically, mentally, socially, and financially—in order to be balanced individuals. God expects us to responsibly manage our beings and every resource that He has placed into our hands.

It takes desire, decision, determination, and discipline to become a good steward. You must be able to see yourself where you are and reason within yourself whether your present lifestyle is working for your good. Is it profitable?

It takes desire, decision, determination, and discipline to become a good steward.

When you see yourself, you must decide with a very strong determination that you are going to get out from where you are and do everything necessary to become better. In the process of doing that, you will have to break some cycles and drop some habits that you have been bound by for years, some of which you may have inherited. Then you can get into a disciplined lifestyle by using the Word of God and prayer as the foundation for managing your life. You can and will never go wrong by applying biblical principles to your lifestyle.

I became a Christian in my teens, and I fellowshipped with the Pentecostals. When I joined them, I noticed that they were an incredibly happy and contented people. They were always in church when the doors opened; very few people would miss service. They loved to pray, fast, and study the Word. I coveted that lifestyle because **I wanted to become** all that God required of me. So, I purposed in my heart that I was going to discipline myself to wake up at 5:00 a.m. in the morning, and I spent time in the Word and prayer before bed at nights.

There was a time, before marriage, that I took the Psalmist David's example by waking up at midnight to give God thanks (Ps. 119:62). I also practiced redirecting my thoughts from situations that I encountered during the day to think on God and His goodness toward me and to sing praises unto Him. At first, it was not easy, but with determination, prayer became a delight to me and no longer a duty. Because of my understanding of what prayer is, I take great delight in encouraging believers in the way of it. As a pastor, my frequent words of encouragement (to the body) are to develop a relationship with

There is no relationship without communication.

God; communicate with Him. There is no relationship without communication.

You may ask, am I perfect? No, definitely not! **My desire to become** all that God requires of me is the driving force. Today, I still maintain my prayer life. I'm up at 5:00 a.m., and I spend time with God at nights. Instead of the TV, I turn on my Bible and let it speak to my spirit while I sleep. I play the Bible and worship music in my home to saturate the atmosphere. Of course, I do have TV time, but I try to live a balanced life. This is a lifestyle to be cultivated. Your desire must be intertwined with decision, discipline, and determination. Every day you wake up, you must choose that which will aid your desire to become.

> *Every day you wake up, you must choose that which will aid your desire to become.*

When we hear stories of people who have worked hard to become a success or even look at movies of people who built great companies, when they think of retiring or are about to die, they always make their successor the person who is the most responsible. It may be a younger son, a daughter, or maybe even an individual who is not a blood relative. Why? Because the individual has displayed the best stewardship skills and is sure to carry on the legacy for generations.

Just imagine you are a parent of a twenty-five-year-old. You are about to journey away from home for six months, so you open a bank account and ensure you have placed sufficient funds in there to take care of the home completely and all the overhead expenses, including food. All the child must do is maintain the cleanliness of the house and make sure the bills are paid on time. After six months, you return to find all the mail stacked up, none of the bills paid, and the bank threatening to repossess your house. And to make matters worse, the account that you gave your child access to is overdrawn. What would your reaction be? You expected that twenty-five-year-old to be a good steward of the resources you gave him or her access to, but now you are angry and disappointed. Imagine how God feels when He looks at us with so many gifts and talents that He has bestowed upon us and we either do nothing with them to glorify Him or we use them to glorify the devil.

Back to the scripture Luke 16:1-4. In it, the rich man is Christ. The steward was accused of wasting the rich man's goods and was called to give an account. Verse 2 says, "And he called him, and said unto him, how is it that I hear this of thee? Give an account of thy stewardship; for thou mayest be no longer steward."

If you were called to give an account today, would you be found guilty of wasting the resources that God has invested in you, of sitting there and doing absolutely nothing with the gifts and talents that God has bestowed upon you?

God has called us into a life that is operative and productive. He has not called us unto stagnancy nor impotence.

> *God has called us into a life that is operative and productive. He has not called us unto stagnancy nor impotence.*

John 15:1-2 and 8 says, "I am the true vine, and my Father is the husbandman. Every branch in me that beareth not fruit he taketh away: and every branch that beareth fruit, he purgeth it, that it may bring forth more fruit. (verse 8) Herein is my father glorified, that ye bear much fruit; so shall ye be my disciples." It is noticeably clear that God is not glorified through an unproductive life. If you are not producing, it means you have chosen the stance of stagnancy and impotence, thus proving yourself worthless. Given the fact that you and I have been engrafted into the body of Christ, we should seek to glorify God by being productive. God expects that from us!

> *It is noticeably clear that God is not glorified through an unproductive life.*

STEWARDSHIP

Stewardship of our total man: spiritual, physical, mental, social, and financial

As we touch each of the five aspects, we must understand every detail thoroughly in order to effectively make adjustments that will impact us for the rest of our lives. Where there is no understanding, it is impossible to apply change.

> *Where there is no understanding, it is impossible to apply change.*

With a sick body, you will never be able to effectively perform the will of God. With a mind that is outside of God's control, you will never please God. With a defective social life or broken relationships, you will be living in discontent, and with financial issues, you will be in a state of frustration. This wholeness we seek is a state of maturity, not perfection. It is growing into a place of maturity that when you are challenged in these areas of your life, you will be able to deal with them from the standpoint of victory, which is the Word of God. You will be in a place of peace and sobriety and will not be overwhelmed nor overcome by your situation.

In 1 Thessalonians 5:23, Paul said, "And the very God of peace sanctify you wholly; and I pray God your whole spirit and soul and body be preserved blameless unto the coming of our Lord Jesus Christ."

Paul was exhorting the church to prepare for the coming of the Lord Jesus Christ, and as they prepared, they learned how they needed to conduct themselves. You may notice that Paul started the verse with "and." He was letting the church know that if they followed the instructions in the previous verses, God Himself would keep them sanctified, not just spiritually but in all aspects because man is a spirit. He has a soul, and he lives in a body, which allows him to have legal access on earth. Then Paul added, "And I pray God that your whole man: spirit, soul and body be preserved [saved from injury, destruction or decay, kept or defended from evil (1828 dictionary)]." Can you feel the passion in Paul's prayer?

Let us start with the:

Spiritual

John 4:24 says, "God is a Spirit: and they that worship him must worship him in spirit and in truth."

Job 32:8 says, "But there is a spirit in man: and the inspiration of the of the almighty giveth them understanding."

Genesis 2:7 says, "And the Lord God formed man of the dust of the ground, and breathe into his nostrils the breath of life, and man became a living soul."

God is a Spirit, and when God breathed into man, it was His Spirit that He was imparting into man to give him life and to bring man into a level of communication with Him. God created us a spirit with a soul and placed us to live in a body.

Proverbs 20:27 says, "The spirit of man is the candle of the Lord, searching all the inward parts of the belly." The NIV version says, "The human spirit is the lamp of the Lord that sheds light on one's inmost being." The sole purpose of a lamp or candle is to give light and dispel darkness. You may notice that when God created man, He used part of Himself, which was His Spirit (He breathed into man, and man became), but He made man's body (the container for His Spirit) from the dust of the earth. Therefore, you may notice that this body, made from the dust of the earth, craves for everything on this earth/in this world, while the spirit yearns for the things of God. The only way that you and I can become what God desires of us is to allow His Spirit in us to be the dominant force.

> *The only way that you and I can become what God desires of us is to allow His Spirit in us to be the dominant force.*

When Adam sinned, our spirit died, but Jesus came and died to cause us to be alive again. Galatians 5:16-17 and 25 says, "This I say then, Walk in the Spirit, and ye shall not fulfill the lust of the flesh. (verse 17) For the flesh lusteth against the Spirit, and the Spirit against the flesh: and these are contrary the one to the other: so that ye cannot do the things that ye would. (verse 25) If we live in the Spirit, let us also walk in the Spirit."

Our spirit is the most important part of our being because it is the part of us that God makes connection with. Your body is important because that is the only legal access you and I have to interact on the earth and with this world. Our bodies house our spirits, and that's why it's of major importance to take care of the body.

The things of the spirit can only be spiritually discerned. You will never be able to see in the spirit realm with your eyes of flesh.

If you notice, God created all the plants, all the animals, and everything that makes up the earth. But the only part of creation He breathed into was man.

> *The things of the spirit can only be spiritually discerned. You will never be able to see in the spirit realm with your eyes of flesh.*

His intention was to be able to relate to man and have man be able to relate to Him. God's sole purpose was to have relationship with us.

Mankind has fallen so far from God that he majors on the natural level, the flesh. Instead of activating that relationship with God, man tries to do all things in his own power.

We pray and tell God of the problem, but we don't trust Him to take care of it. So, we get out of our prayer rooms and go devising ways and means to fix our situations ourselves, leaving God completely out of the equation. Then we end up in extremely chaotic situations.

Jesus said in the book of John 6:63, "It is the spirit that quickeneth; the flesh profiteth nothing." In simple terms, Jesus was saying to major on your spirit life because there is no profit in the flesh. Your flesh is dust, and to dust it will return. What matters is the Spirit that God breathes into you. There needs to be a bridge between the spiritual and the natural—the Holy Spirit.

When you understand that life is the imparting of Spirit into mortal man and death is the departing of Spirit from man, then you will understand the importance of your spirit. When your body dies, your spirit continues to live because it was God-breathed.

> *When you understand that life is the imparting of Spirit into mortal man and death is the departing of Spirit from man, then you will understand the importance of your spirit.*

We must be fortified in our spirits in order to dominate the spirit realm. Then we will be able to clearly discern, accurately diagnose, and strategically address situations from a kingdom standpoint.

> *We must be fortified in our spirits in order to dominate the spirit realm. Then we will be able to clearly discern, accurately diagnose, and strategically address situations from a kingdom standpoint.*

As an example, Jesus (God the Son) manifested Himself in the flesh and showed us how we ought to live this life that God created us for. Just consider the fact that He was Himself God the Son, but He prayed, He fasted, and He spent time in the temple studying the Word. He loved (Mary, Martha, and brother Lazarus), He exercised compassion, He healed the sick, He raised the dead, and He gave. All of this was done to show man how to live this relationship with God the Father.

Following Jesus's example is quite easy. The difficulty arises when man tries to alter the example and pattern that Jesus laid down. As someone who loves to cook, I never fully follow a recipe. I always try to put a twist on it with the intention of getting a better flavor/result.

> *Following Jesus's example is quite easy. The difficulty arises when man tries to alter the example and pattern that Jesus laid down.*

We should never try to put our twist on the pattern that Jesus laid down in the gospels. Let us go back to them and follow the pattern that Jesus laid closely, looking at His prayer life, Word life, and fasting life.

PRAYER LIFE

In Luke 18:1, Jesus said, "Men ought always to pray, and not to faint. It is necessary for them to pray consistently and never quit (MSG). They ought always to pray and not to turn coward (faint, loose heart and give up) (AMP)."

To effectively carry out a task, one must understand the instructions that go with it.

What is prayer?

Prayer in its simplest term is communication with God—**being able to talk to God and listen** to what He has to say to you in response. It is exposing oneself in the presence of God and giving Him access into your life to interfere in your affairs. It is having a relationship with God the Father and the privilege of having direct communication with Him.

> *To effectively carry out a task, one must understand the instructions that go with it.*

What prayer is not:

It is not a burden; it is coming to bring your burdens to God. It is not a task; it is putting God on task on your behalf. It is not a duty; it should become a delight.

Why pray?

When God created man, He left in man a void that only He can fulfill. Haven't you noticed that man is seeking after a god? Man is always looking for something or someone to worship, but not everyone chooses the Almighty God. There are countless religions on this earth and many gods

Spiritual

that man has set up for himself because that void needs to be filled.

Our first example of prayer is Jesus. He was God the Son, but He maintained communication with the Father as He walked on earth. Jesus did nothing without the Father's consent.

Mark 1:35-39: Jesus got up a great while before dawn.
John 11:41-42: Jesus prayed in the day.
Matthew 14:23: Jesus prayed at night.
Luke 6:12: Jesus prayed all night.

Jesus prayed everywhere: Mark 6:46 (on the mountain); Mark 15:34 and Luke 23:34-36 (on the cross)

Prayer should be the believer's lifestyle.

Prayer should be a delight to us and not a duty. It should give us pleasure to sit in our Father's presence. Talking to our Father God should become a priority among our everyday activity, but you and I must grow in love with Him.

Prayer should be a delight to us and not a duty. It should give us pleasure to sit in our Father's presence.

STEWARDSHIP

I have been in love, and I know that when two persons grow to love each other, they talk unceasingly, and they make big sacrifices to spend time in each other's presence. No matter what resistance they come up against, they will defy it all, even if it becomes painful, just to be with each other. When you are in love with God, prayer becomes easy. You want to talk with Him. You want to know what is on His mind concerning you.

1 Thessalonians 5:17 says, "Pray without ceasing (be unceasing and persistent in prayer)" (AMP). All people have something in their everyday lives that they have trained themselves to do. For example, some people must start the day with a cup of coffee. Some start the day by reading a newspaper or looking at the news, while others get of their bed and get down on their knees, etc. Whatever you practice over a period of time becomes a habit. It becomes part of you.

You should not just pray when you are visited by trouble, but you should become a person of prayer. Prayer should be your nature because sometimes, it can become difficult to pray in a time of trouble and grief. You can only speak in your heart like Hannah did in 1 Samuel 1:13. In these times, God understands because you are accustomed to being in His presence. Jesus did not just pray to have a miracle performed or when He needed the Father to do something. He led a consistent life of prayer.

Spiritual

2 Chronicles 7:14 says, "If my people which are called by my name, shall humble themselves and pray…"

It takes humility to pray. When people have it all, they become proud and see no need to pray. As a matter of fact, they do not even give God credit for the health, strength, and wisdom He lent them to attain it.

> *It takes humility to pray.*

Ephesians 6:18, says, "Praying always with all prayer and supplication in the Spirit, and watching thereunto with all perseverance and supplication for all saints." The verse says "all prayers," meaning that there are different types of prayers, and you need to know which prayer applies when you get into God's presence.

Example (gotquestions.org):

The Prayer of Faith: James 5:15, "And the prayer of faith shall save the sick, and the Lord shall raise him up."

The Prayer of Agreement or Corporate Prayer: Acts 1:14, 2:42, "These all continued with one accord in prayer and supplication, with the women, and Mary the mother of Jesus, and with his brethren. And they continued steadfastly in the Apostles' doctrine and fellowship, and in breaking of bread and in prayers." The disciples all joined together constantly in prayer.

The Prayer of Supplication or Request: Philippians 4:6 and Ephesians 6:18, "Be careful for nothing; but in every thing by prayer and supplication with thanksgiving let your requests be made known unto God. Praying always with all prayer and supplication in the spirit." It means that we can take our requests to God.

The Prayer of Thanksgiving: Philippians 4:6, "Be careful for nothing; but in every thing by prayer and supplication with thanksgiving let your requests be made known unto God." God expects us to show gratitude for everything that He does in our lives. Therefore, He always expects us to return with thanksgiving.

The Prayer of Worship: Psalms 29:1-2, "Give unto the Lord, O ye mighty, give unto the Lord glory and strength. Give unto the Lord the glory due unto his name; worship the Lord in the beauty of holiness." This prayer is directed to God; you tell Him who He is and what He is to you.

The Prayer of Consecration: Mathew 26:39, "And he went a little further, and fell on his face, and prayed, saying, O my Father, if it be possible, let this cup pass from me: nevertheless not as I will, but as thou wilt." It is a prayer where you set yourself apart to follow God's will.

The Prayer of Intercession: 1 Timothy 2:1 and, very importantly, John 17. This is where you come to God on behalf of others. Before Jesus left the earth, He interceded for all those who were with Him and all who would become a part of the body of Christ.

The Prayer of Imprecation: Psalms 7, 55, 69. Psalm 7:6 says, "Arise, O Lord, in thy anger, lift up thyself because of the rage of mine enemies: and awake for me to the judgement that thou hast commanded." These prayers are prayed to invoke God's judgement on the wicked and avenge the righteous.

Prayer should precede everything in the believer's life. If you pray before studying the Word of God, you will get understanding. If you pray before deciding, you will receive God's perspective. If you pray before moving, you will receive God's direction. If you find it difficult to pray, follow the pattern of prayer that Jesus left us in Matthew 6:9-13. Many use it as a prayer, but it is a pattern. It starts with, "After this manner therefore pray ye..."

Prayer should precede everything in the believer's life.

Fasting Life

Fasting, for the believer, is deliberately abstaining from food while you position yourself in prayer and the Word of God in order to receive instruction and guidance for a life situation. There are, however, different types of fasts.

Matthew 4:1-4 says Jesus fasted for forty days and nights:

> It was after Jesus' forty days of fasting that the devil came to tempt Him with the lust of the flesh, the lust of the eyes and the pride of life. In those forty days, His flesh which was the human part of Him was totally subdued to His spirit. Therefore, when Satan came to tempt Him, he was able to overcome. Immediately after this, Jesus started His ministry on earth.

Reasons for Fasting

1. To overcome temptation–fasting kills the flesh but empowers the spirit (Matt. 4:3-11).

2. To receive a direction, instruction, word, or order from God (Esther 4:15-17). For the safety of the Jews, God positioned her as queen in the kingdom. She had no right to be queen as she was a Jew. It was not her time to go unto the king. She had not been called to his chamber, so she fasted. Deuteronomy 9:9-18: Moses fasted forty days and received the Ten Commandments from God, our Father.

Spiritual

3. For God's intervention in your situation (Dan. 10:1-13). Daniel fasted for three weeks (twenty-one days) for an answer to prayer. He also needed clarity, so he sought God in fasting and prayer and got his answer.

It was about my third year as a believer when I desired more of God and went into five days of prayer and fasting. The Lord gave me a scripture from Isaiah 58:12 and told me that He would use me to build old waste places and raise foundations and make me a repairer of breaches and a restorer of paths to dwell in. I never understood what that meant until I arrived in the state of Massachusetts and God placed me among a people with kingdom vision.

Some of the most important decisions that I have made in my life came when God instructed me in a time of prayer and fasting. I did not go to a prophet nor a psychic for direction, just God. When I look back to where I came from and where I am today, I give glory to God. It is through my personal experiences that I am moved to motivate believers to develop a prayer life, which is of most importance to a believer.

When my husband and I received confirmation from God and started dating, the first thing we established in our lives was prayer and a specific day of the week for fasting. This year, we will be married for seven years, and this is our foundation on which we stand. When we arrive at difficult areas in our lives, we resort to prayer and fasting, and God has never failed us.

Fasting must be as God-ordained (Isa. 58:6-13). One must have God's perspective when entering a period of fasting.

Word Life

We go to school to get a certificate, a diploma, or a degree. We work hard to attain that because it's important to show the world our achievements. 2 Timothy 2:15 says, "Study to show thyself approved unto God." There are heights and depths and dimensions that we can attain in God, but we must know what the Word says about us. The Word of God is the bread of the Christian life. Just as you need the natural food to sustain your body, so you need the Word of God to sustain your spirit. It is food for your spirit. The Word of God is also our defense in spiritual combat. When Jesus was tempted in Matthew 4, He defended himself with the Word. If you do not know the Word, you will not be able to defend yourself in spiritual combat.

> *If you do not know the Word, you will not be able to defend yourself in spiritual combat.*

Psalm 119:11 says, "Thy word have I hid in my heart…" Having a Bible in your possession is a good thing, but it is better to memorize the Word of God so that in a time of trouble, the Holy Spirit can recall to your memory the most fitting scripture for your situation.

John 14:26 says, "He shall teach you all things, and bring all things to your remembrance, whatsoever I have said unto you."

The Holy Spirit can only remind you of what you already know. Therefore, increase your knowledge of God's Word.

The Holy Spirit can only remind you of what you already know. Therefore, increase your knowledge of God's Word.

Psalm 119:130 says, "The entrance of thy words giveth light." One of the things we must realize is that there is a scripture in the Bible that will remedy any situation that you and I will ever encounter as we go through this life. The Bible is like an app store, whereby we just need to find the right app for our situation.

John 8:31-32 and John 17:17 say the Word is truth. The Word sets free. God's Word is the foundation of truth, and when you attain knowledge of it, it will bring you freedom in any situation or circumstance that you encounter in this life.

It is good to have all the degrees and certificates that you can attain, but nothing that you attain in this life can ever equal to the knowledge of God's Word.

What is your relationship with God right now? Do you make time to have fellowship with Him? Is God really an important part of your life, or do you just call Him up in a time of trouble? Is prayer a duty to you or a delight? How much time do you spend studying the Bible? Do you only open it when you go to church? Do you have an appetite for the things of God, or are you just going through the motions? Always remember that God is a jealous God, and He desires always to be number one and second to none.

LET US PRAY:

Father, I come to You today in view of the life pattern that Jesus laid down in the gospels. Lord, I repent for not following the pattern of life that was laid down for me. I ask You, Lord, to forgive me for my adjustment of the pattern, my alteration of the pattern, my twist on the pattern.

Father, I understand that You created man the highest of all Your creation and among all living creatures. It was only man that You breathed Your breath into. I understand that my existence is of great importance to You because Your intention is to have fellowship with me and that I live a life glorifying You. I understand that in order to please

Spiritual

You, I must maintain a prayer life, a fasting life, and a life of studying Your Word.

Today, I ask You based on Your Word in John 6:44, which says, "No man can come to me except the Father which hath sent me draws him." Lord, draw me unto You and give me a hunger for Your Word, a hunger for fasting, and a thirst for prayer and Your presence. I ask You, Lord, to restore me unto Your desired intention so that I can serve You in spirit and in truth, in Jesus's name.

I come against every spirit that has been an influence in my life, in Jesus's name. I call them by name: prayerlessness, lack of studying the Word of God, procrastination, lackadaisicalness, excuses, laziness, sleep, and slumber. I bind you all and shut down your enterprises. Catch fire and burn to ash right now, in Jesus's name. I call into my life the spirit of prayer, the spirit of worship, and the spirit of love for the study of God's Word right now, in Jesus's name. Lord, stir up Your spirit in me. Restore unto me the joy of Your salvation and the joy of serving Jesus and renew a right spirit within me, in Jesus's name. Amen.

And according to 1 Thessalonians 5:23: "And the very God of peace sanctify you wholly; and I pray that your whole spirit and soul and body be preserved blameless unto the coming of our Lord Jesus Christ." Amen.

Physical

1 Corinthians 6:19-20: "What? Know ye not that your body is the temple of the Holy Ghost, which is in you, which ye have of God, and ye are not your own? For ye are bought with a price: therefore, glorify God in your body, and in your spirit, which are God's."

1 Corinthians 3:16: "Know ye not that you are the temple of God?"

1 Corinthians 6:15: "Know ye not that your bodies are the members of Christ?"

Romans 12:1: "I beseech you therefore, brethren, by the mercies of God, that ye present your bodies a living sacrifice, holy, acceptable unto God, which is your reasonable service."

Romans 6:12: "Let not sin therefore reign in your mortal body, that you should obey it in the lusts thereof."

First, we must understand that we are not our own; God paid the price of the blood of His Son Jesus for us. The bodies that you and I live in are the only things that give us legal rights to operate on this earth. Without a body, we will cease to exist physically.

How we treat our bodies and what we do with our bodies affects our Father and our Lord Jesus Christ.

> *Without a body, we will cease to exist physically.*

> *We need the wisdom of God to effectively maintain this temple.*

We need the wisdom of God to effectively maintain this temple. Every building must be maintained. Eating, drinking, resting, exercising, and maintaining proper hygiene are important elements of self-care. What we put into and how we treat our bodies matters.

We need to watch what we eat and how we eat. We need to watch what we drink. We need to watch our excessive use of sugar and salt. Many foods are delightful to the taste, but they are destructive to our bodies. We are living in a "fast food" age, where people prefer to go through the drive-thru or order in instead of turning on the stove to cook a fresh, healthy meal. What we do not realize is that a large portion of food on the shelf is fixed for fast sale, not for good health. As the body of Christ, we need to be wiser. I am not saying that you can't treat yourself or family to some fast food or order in every now and again, but that should not

Physical

be your lifestyle. We should get back to the days of cooking healthy meals.

We have children who are now growing up, and all they eat is junk. They refuse to eat fruits and vegetables. They will eat pizza or even ice cream for breakfast. Some of them will not even have a drink of water. They would rather have soda or juice. Thus, the rate of obesity is skyrocketing between men, women, and children. What we don't realize is that it's a trick of the enemy to immobilize us, to cut our lives short so that we don't fulfill the calling of God on our lives. Remember in the book of John 10:10, "The thief cometh, not but for to steal, and to kill and to destroy." What the devil doesn't steal, he will kill, and what he fails in killing, he will destroy. Please do not continue to allow bad eating habits to destroy your health and your life. "Bridle your appetite" (Prov. 23:2 MSG). A bridle, according to Merriam Webster's dictionary, is "a headgear with which a horse is governed." This scripture is therefore telling us that we should govern our appetites and take control of them.

Bearing in mind that our bodies are the temples of God, we should put time and effort into our personal hygiene. We should also put time and effort into our dressing. We should always dress to represent the kingdom of God. When people look at us, if they have a question, it should be connected to a positive thought, not a negative one. I always say, "We should set the standard for the world; the world should not set the standard for the church, the body of Christ." The body of Christ should not patronize every style this world produces. 2 Corinthians 6:14-17, with emphasis on verse 17, says, "Wherefore come out from among them, and be ye separate, saith the Lord."

The many sicknesses and diseases that are plaguing the body of Christ today primarily result from bad eating and drinking habits, a lack of exercise, and a lack of sleep. 1 Timothy 4:8 says, "For bodily exercise profiteth little." It means that although the greater profit is in godliness because it prepares you for eternal life in Christ, there is still profit in exercising your physical body. When was the last time you took a nice walk? People get up in the morning and jump into their cars or on the bus to work. They sit at their desks all day, and on their return home, sit again in front of the TV. This is the circle of life, thus resulting in premature aging, sickness, and even death.

It is necessary to give the body adequate rest. The Almighty God showed us an example in Genesis 2:2, which says, "And on the seventh day God ended his work which he had made; and he rested on the seventh day from all his work which he had made." God was showing us that in all labor, we must find time to rest. He is the Almighty, and He really doesn't need rest. But He placed it there for our example so that we would know that we must balance labor with rest. We use this body to make the money we desire, but we must rest this body so that it can be replenished. God created night and day. You work all day and should get adequate sleep at nights. Sleep has great benefits and is a natural healer for the body. It reduces stress and inflammation, it improves memory, it helps in weight loss, it makes you more alert and smarter, it reduces your risk of depression, and so much more. It is said that your heart will be healthier if you get between seven and nine hours of sleep every night (verywellhealth.com). Let's work on improving our times of rest/sleep!

I come from a family of not-slim people on both my mother's and father's sides. Among my siblings and I, we exercise a lot of control when it comes to eating healthy because we understand the importance. There are things that I personally love very much, but I discipline myself in eating them. I shop healthy foods and keep junk out of my home to avoid temptation.

Healing scriptures: Isaiah 53:4-5: "Surely he hath borne our griefs, and carried our sorrows: ye we did esteem him stricken, smitten of God, and afflicted. But he was wounded for our transgressions, he was bruised for our iniquities: the chastisement of our peace was upon him, and with his stripes we are healed."

Exodus 15:26: "And said, if you will diligently hearken to the voice of the Lord thy God, and wilt do that which is right in his sight, and wilt give ear to his commandments, and keep all his statues, I will put none of these diseases upon thee, which I have brought upon the Egyptians: for I am the Lord that healeth thee."

Exodus 23:25: "And ye shall serve the Lord thy God, and he shall bless thy bread, and thy water; and I will take sickness away from the midst of thee."

Psalm 34:19-20: "Many are the afflictions of the righteousness: but the Lord delivereth him out of the them all. He keepeth all his bones: not one of them is broken."

Matthew 8:17: "That it might be fulfilled which was spoken by Esaias the prophet, saying, Himself took our infirmities, and bare our sicknesses."

1 Peter 2:24: "Who his own self bare our sins in his own body on the tree, that we being dead to sins, should live unto righteousness: by whose stripes ye were healed."

Psalm 103:3: "Who forgiveth all thine iniquities; who healeth all thy diseases."

Psalm 107:20: "He sent his word, and healed them, and delivered them from their destructions."

Physical

If you are not physically fit/ready, you can be detrimental to the mission. That can cause chaos in the body of Christ because each one of us has our individual part to play. Just as our physical body has different parts, so are we different parts in the body of Christ, and we must be functioning. You and I do not know how many people are attached to us to be brought into the body of Christ.

Our body as the temple of the Lord means that God lives in us. He does not just visit but has taken up residence in us when we accepted His Son Jesus Christ as our Lord and Savior (1 Cor. 6:19).

Romans 12:2 says, "And be not conformed to this world but be ye transformed by the renewing of your mind." Renewing of your mind will bring transformation in your body. The change must start in your head. We must change the way we think and reprogram our minds for our bodies to fall in alignment.

> *Renewing of your mind will bring transformation in your body. The change must start in your head.*

Romans 12:1 (NIV) says, "Therefore, I urge you, brothers and sisters, in view of God's mercy, to offer your bodies as a living sacrifice, holy and pleasing to God – this is your true and proper worship."

Sacrifice means an act of offering something precious to a deity. We must be able to see our bodies as something precious and that we cannot soil them with fornication, adultery, gluttony, nor any other thing that will cause damage to them. We should make our bodies a daily offering unto God.

That is true and proper worship according to the scripture above. So, let us worship God with our bodies.

1 Corinthians 6:20 (AMP) says, "You were bought with a price. You were actually purchased with the precious blood of Jesus and made his own. So then, honour and glorify God with your body."

If you purchase something, you then become the owner of that thing. No one else has ownership but you. God has bought us. He paid the price of the blood of His Son Jesus. Therefore, He owns you and me. We were bought and are not our own. Whatever you and I do with our bodies, we will be held accountable for it.

1 Corinthians 6:13 (AMP) says, "The body is not intended for sexual immorality, but for the Lord, and the Lord is for the body [to save, sanctify, and raise it again, because of the sacrifice of the cross." According to Webster's dictionary, the word immoral means "conflicting with generally or traditionally held moral principles." It means that the Word of God (the Bible) has set the standard for sex. Sex must take

place within marriage between a man and a woman, and anything outside of that is conflicting with the Word of God.

Romans 6:12 (AMP) says, "Therefore do not let sin reign in your mortal body so that you obey its lust and passion."

Do not allow sin to have royal authority, dominion, nor influence over your life.

> *Do not allow sin to have royal authority, dominion, nor influence over your life.*

It was God's intention to have communion and fellowship with man (the highest being of all creation). When Adam sinned, he broke the relationship, but God so loved man (John 3:16) that He decided to find a way to restore that relationship. God would take the time to come down in the cool of the day to fellowship with Adam in the garden (Gen. 3:8). God enjoyed that because when He created man, He made him in His own image, someone who could communicate with Him. God missed that fellowship, so He decided to devise a way to bring man back to his intended status. He sent His Son Jesus down to earth to interact with man, to get fully acquainted with man, and then to die for man's restoration.

"As many as received him, to them gave the power to become the Sons of God" (John 1:12).

As a human being, you will always be tempted to sin because that's the enemy's strategy against God (to tempt man to sin), but it is how you and I deal with that temptation that is important.

Romans 6:12 says, "Let not sin therefore reign in your mortal body, that ye should obey it in the lusts thereof." Reign means to possess or exercise sovereign power, to rule, or to hold office as chief. Do not allow any type of sin to reign or hold office as chief in your body. God wants to reign because He paid the price for your body. We must understand that all sin is sin, whether it is a white lie, fornication, or murder. Sin does not go by measure or size. Sin is sin.

Do not allow any type of sin to reign or hold office as chief in your body.

Sin does not go by measure or size. Sin is sin.

You must know that because your body is God's temple, you have a right to divine health. Do not accept any kind of sickness in your body because according to Isaiah 53:5, "But he was wounded for our transgressions, he was bruised for our iniquities: the chastisement of our peace was upon him; and with his stripes we are healed." Therefore, every stripe Jesus took represents the sicknesses that are known to man. Tell the devil that Jesus took a stripe so that you could be healed today. Say, "I am healed in Jesus's name!" Let us look at "the chastisement of our peace was upon Him." According to vocabulary.com, chastisement means "reprimand, punishment, beating." To be at peace means you are in a tranquil state of mind. The opposite of peace is noise, disturbance, agitation, war. The coronavirus is presently chastising the peace of the entire world. Its symptoms are restriction, control, suffocation, bondage, hinderance, separation, interruption to normality, fear, and anxiety, resulting in death. The peace of nations is being chastised because as the disease spreads, the death toll is rising. In all of this, we must remember that Jesus took thirty-nine stripes. If you do not have peace of mind, you will eventually end up being physically ill.

When you look at your body, are you satisfied with your appearance? Do you have control of your appetite? Do you have a higher craving for the foods that are detrimental to your health? What are you willing to do, and how far are you willing to go to bring a change to your physical appearance? Are you leading a moral life in accordance with the Word of God?

LET US PRAY:

Lord, 1 Corinthians 3:16-17 says, "Know ye not that ye are the temple of God, and that the Spirit of God dwelleth in you? If any man defiles the temple of God, him shall God destroy; for the temple of God is holy, which temple ye are." I understand that my body is Your temple. You do not only own me, but You live here and paid a price for me. So today, I repent of my disregard of Your ownership and lordship of my body. I ask You to forgive me for every sin that I have committed against this body, Your temple. I receive Your forgiveness, and I ask You today for the wisdom to effectively maintain good stewardship over this body, Your temple.

I place my eating and drinking habits before You. Help me to bridle my appetite according to Proverbs 23:2 (NIV). Help me, Lord, to not be gluttonous in my eating. Help me to maintain a balanced diet and to nurture good eating and drinking habits, in Jesus's name. Help me to apply wisdom whenever I sit to eat, according to 1 Corinthians 6:13 (AMP).

I understand that my body is not intended for sexual immorality. I desire to please You in my body, Lord. So today, I renounce all unclean practices of immorality. I dedicate this body to You, Father. I ask You to strengthen me in Your Word so that I can bring my body into subjection as a living sacrifice to You daily. Lord, I give You ownership over this body. Lord, reign over this body and accept Lordship over it, in Jesus's name.

I pray for healing in my body right now, in Jesus's name. I come against every sickness and disease that would try to attach itself to my body or lodge in my body, in Jesus's name.

Every disease that have been running down through my family lineage must die now, in Jesus's name. Sugar diabetes, high blood pressure, cancer, heart disease, liver disease, lung disease, brain disease, blood disease—you must die now, in Jesus's name.

I break every generational curse that would try to attach itself to my body and destroy every pattern from generations that would try to influence me against honoring God in my body and with my body, in Jesus's name. I break cycles of going back to old habits, in Jesus's name. I command the healing power of God to flow through my body right now, impacting my body from the crown of my head through my brain, blood, arteries, veins, and every organ of my body. I command the healing power of God through my joints and marrow, hands and legs, down to the tips of my toes, in Jesus's name. I declare healing in this body, God's temple, in Jesus's name. Amen. Resurrection power flow through me right now, in Jesus's name. Amen!

I decree and declare that my body is the temple of God and is under the Lordship of Jesus Christ. **I decree and declare** that according to Romans 12:1 (NIV), I will give God true and proper worship by offering my body as a living sacrifice to God daily. **I decree and declare** that I am healed, in Jesus's name. No sickness, no disease, and no infirmity shall dwell in my body.

STEWARDSHIP

I decree and declare that I will give this body adequate rest because God our Father worked for six days and rested on the seventh, an indication that man ought to work but take time to rest (Gen. 2:2). I will rest this body, in Jesus's name. Amen.

Mental

We want to examine the mind, which is a powerful aspect of the human being. Someone once said, "The mind is a powerful thing to waste."

We really cannot underestimate the power of the mind because the mind is like the control tower of the human being. According to Google, the mind has three functions—thoughts, feelings, and desires, and these three functions are what gives human beings the most difficulty throughout their lifetimes if they are not submitted to Almighty God's control.

> And do not be conformed to this world [any longer with its superficial values and customs], but be transformed and progressively changed [as you mature spiritually] by the renewing of your mind [focusing on godly values and ethical attitudes], so that you may prove [for yourselves] what the will of God is, that which is good and

acceptable and perfect [in His plan and purpose for you].

- Romans 12:2 (AMP)

Paul's command is, "Do not be conformed to this world **but** be transformed and progressively changed by the renewing of your mind." It is impossible to be conformed to this world and be transformed into the mind of God at the same time. The mind of God is light, and the world with its system is darkness.

"Renew your mind focusing on godly values and ethical attitudes." Renewing your mind will not be successful if your focus is off. As a child of God, you must be focused on the things of God and on His kingdom. Renewing your mind is constantly purging your mind from the thoughts that the devil gives you and replacing them with thoughts that are in line with Philippians 4:8, which says, "Finally my brethren, whatsoever things are true, whatsoever things are honest, whatsoever things are just, whatsoever things are pure, whatsoever things are lovely, whatsoever things are of good report; if there be any virtue, and if there be any praise, think on these things." It means our every thought must be tested through the above

> *"Renew your mind focusing on godly values and ethical attitudes."*

scripture, and if it fails, then it must be discarded and is not qualified to be entertained.

You may be saying right now that this is difficult or maybe impossible, but I want to assure you that it is possible. The secret is easy—practice. Luke 1:37 says, "For with God nothing shall be impossible."

The second part says, "And progressively changed by the renewing of your mind." It is sad to watch believers strive to make progress on their jobs, in their families, at school and in society, doing everything possible to get to the top and win, but when it comes to God, they refuse to make progress. They do not want to thrive because there is no tangible paycheck at the end of the month.

A constant renewing of the mind will bring progressive change and transformation.

> *A constant renewing of the mind will bring progressive change and transformation.*

We must start with the mind first because if the mind is not in its rightful position in Christ—focusing on the kingdom—then the body will not line up. There must be a mind alignment first.

Every action, reaction, decision, choice, etc., starts with a thought. No one just gets up and commits an act, whether good or bad. A murderer starts with a thought. The root thought could be jealousy, which develops into hatred and eventually leads to murder. A thief starts with a thought, the root being covetousness—"I want that!" Then he plots a way to be able to obtain that thing. The adulterer/fornicator starts with a thought, of which the root is lust. No matter what the action/execution, it begins with a thought. That is why 2 Corinthians 10:5 says, "Casting down imaginations, and every thigh thing that exalteth itself against the knowledge of God and bringing into captivity every thought to the obedience of Christ."

When someone commits suicide, it starts with a thought, which at the root could be rejection. Rejection of oneself may be as a result of a situation one has been through or rejection by others, which has brought him or her into a depressed and lonely state. The thought says, "No one loves you. No one cares, so get rid of yourself." The imagination comes into play and says, "Here is an easy way out," and after entertaining it for a period, that imagination develops into a stronghold that drives one to execute. If you ever arrive at this place in your life, you should seek some spiritual or professional help.

You cannot play with any negative thought for any given time. When the enemy sends a thought and it does not line up with the Word of God, you must cast it down and bring it into captivity. A thought is easy to manage. Get rid of it in the thought stage because if you entertain it, it will grow and become an imagination.

In the imagination stage, you start seeing yourself in the situation. You begin to enjoy what you see, and so you continue to entertain until it becomes a stronghold. It is difficult to get rid of a stronghold. You need divine deliverance at that stage because you cannot manage it alone.

You must realize that behind every negative thought is a spirit—a lying spirit whose intention is to kill, steal, and destroy you and your destiny.

> *You must realize that behind every negative thought is a spirit*

Many are bound, enslaved by past experiences, past hurts, past pains—just bound by the past. And the enemy feeds them with the thought daily that they cannot move pass this. 2 Corinthians 5:17 says, "Therefore if any man be in Christ, he is a new creature: old things are passed away and behold, all things are become new."

> *We must take God at the surface value of His Word.*

We must take God at the surface value of His Word. The situation is in your past, not your present, not your future—you are in Christ. That situation has passed away. Allow the Lord to emancipate your mind. If you continue to think in the past, you will continue to be a victim of how you think.

Trade with the Lord! Give Him the situation, and allow Him to reprogram your mind. He will give you the mind of Christ, and you will be able to see yourself past this.

2 Corinthians 2:16 says, "...but we have the mind of Christ." When we accept Jesus as Lord, He gives us His mind, which is found in His Word, the Bible. Every believer ought to walk in the mind of Christ. If Christ gave us His mind, it is our responsibility to allow it to prevail in us. You may ask, "What is the mind of Christ?" Well, it is simple. If your thoughts do not line up with the Word of God, then it is not the mind of Christ.

Romans 8:6 says, "For to be carnally minded is death." Verse 7 (NIV) says, "The mind governed by the flesh is hostile to God; it does not submit to God's law nor can it do so." According to Merriam Webster's dictionary, the word hostile means "openly opposed or resisting, showing unfriendly feelings, enemy."

Walking in the flesh is walking in the dictates of your own mind. It is walking in the way where your thoughts are leading you and not according to God's Word. When you walk in your own mindset, you are walking in hostility toward God. You are openly opposing and resisting Him and walking in enmity with Him.

You cannot tame a carnal mind. You must dispel it.

> *You cannot tame a carnal mind. You must dispel it.*

What thoughts are you presently entertaining concerning God, yourself, and your past or present situation? Are your thoughts leading you to a decision that is in line with the Word of God? Do you think that God is being glorified with the decision that you have made or are about to make? Let us take a moment right here to pause and think deeply about it.

I know of a Christian woman who was married to a pastor. He would go to work every day and sit in the company of co-workers who would entice him with their adulterous lifestyle. This man would come home and relay to his wife the stories told to him. In response, his wife would admonish him to stop sitting in these men's company except if he was willing to shine his light to them so that they could see their way out of their mess. Instead of doing the right thing, that husband continued to sit and enjoy the ungodly company of his coworkers, and over a period of time, he became like them and fell into the same adulterous lifestyle. His co-workers sowed the seeds, and he spent time thinking on them until those thoughts took over his mind and emotions, and he became a victim. Through this, he lost his family, his reputation, and his ministry. The thoughts we entertain can result in our destruction.

How is your mind? Do you find yourself disturbed by your past? Are you in a situation right now where you feel pressured to do something that you know is contrary to the Word of God? Are you halted between two opinions? Is it difficult to concentrate on the Word of God?

> *The thoughts we entertain can result in our destruction.*

LET US PRAY:

Father, in the name of Jesus Christ, I come before You. Lord, I confess that I have problems with my mind. Lord, when I examine myself, I realize that I have not been a good steward of the thoughts that I entertain and allow to take root in my mind. My thoughts keep pulling me back into my past, making me relive the pain like my situation just happened. So today, I bring my mind to You. I understand that according to 2 Corinthians 5:17, "I am in Christ and I am a new creature, old things are passed away and you have made all things new." Therefore, I renounce that situation of my past (**name it**).

Today, I take the freedom that Christ died to give me, and I cut my mind loose from every residue of my past that keeps lingering and causing my mind to stray. I uproot thoughts that have kept me bound and stunted me spiritually over the years. According to Romans 8:7 (NIV), "The carnal mind is hostile towards God: And does not submit to the law of God."

Lord, it is my desire to live in unity with You, not in enmity. According to 2 Corinthians 10:5, "I cast down every imagination and every high thing that exalteth itself against the knowledge of God, and I bring into captivity every thought to the obedience of Christ. I bring every contrary thought into captivity."

Lord, thank you that You have given me power over my thoughts so that I can take captive every thought that is contrary to Your Word. **I decree and declare**, according to 1 Corinthians 2:16, that I have the mind of Christ. I operate with a kingdom mindset and in the character of the Lord Jesus because I have the mind of Christ.

I thank you for the guideline of Philippians 4:8. **I shall** think on things that are true. **I shall** think on things that are honest. **I shall** think on things that are just. **I shall** think on things that are pure. **I shall** think on things that are lovely. **I shall** think on things that are of good report. Lord, I give You the Lordship over my mind. Thank you for accepting Lordship and reprogramming my mind, in Jesus's name. Amen.

Social

Human beings were created to be social. That's why the only thing that God said was not good was for Adam to be alone (Gen. 2:18). "God said I will make him a help meet. Then God told them to be fruitful and multiply and replenish" (Gen. 1:28).

He did not only give man a mate, but He gave every species of animal a mate. However, His one intention was that He would be glorified. Genesis 2:15 says, "And the Lord God took the man, and put him into the garden of Eden to dress it and to keep it." God gave Adam chores so that he would not be idle nor unproductive. He placed him in the garden of Eden to dress it and keep it. Verse 19 says, "And out of the ground the Lord God formed every beast of the field, and every fowl of the air; and brought them unto Adam to see what he would call them: and whatsoever Adam called every living creature, that was the name thereof." God gave Adam the responsibility for naming the animals.

God gave Adam his wife, "And the rib, which the Lord God had taken from man, made he a woman, and brought her unto the man. And Adam said, This is now bone of my bones, and flesh of my flesh: she shall be called woman, because she was taken out of Man. Therefore shall a man leave his father and his mother, and shall cleave unto his wife: and they shall be one flesh" (Gen. 2:22-24. God established the fact that a man should leave his father and mother and cleave to his wife. At that time, there were only two people, Adam and Eve, but God wanted to establish the fact that a man marrying a woman should be as one person.

God came down in the cool of the day to have fellowship with Adam. So there was a time for work, a time for play (with his wife), and a time reserved for fellowship and communion with God. God wants us to live a balanced life, but everything must be in its proper perspective with one aim, and that is to glorify God.

We cannot be all heavenly-focused and no earthly good. Because while we fix our eyes on heaven, we still dwell on earth. We also cannot allow ourselves to get so caught up with our jobs or families, however, that we make no time available for fellowship with God. That is the demonstration of an off-balanced life. There is nothing nor anyone that should take pre-eminence over our time of fellowship with God.

Proverbs 18:24: "A man of friends must shew himself friendly."

Social

Proverbs 17:17: "A friend loveth at all times."

Proverbs 27:17: "Iron sharpeneth iron; so a man sharpeneth the countenance of his friend."

We must nurture good relationships and discard toxic ones. Ephesians 5:11 says, "And have no fellowship with the unfruitful works of darkness but rather reprove them." There are people who are toxic. When they come into your presence, whatever they have deposited in you sends you to repent after they leave because it was not godly. There are others who drain you. They are just there to take but make no significant deposits in your life. If you cannot help them to improve and to come up to your level, or if they cannot help you to improve, then you need to decide to cut them out of your life.

We must nurture good relationships and discard toxic ones.

Everyone who comes into your life is not there for a lifetime. God may send someone for a day, a week, a month, or maybe a year or few years, and some may just stop by for a few minutes or hours. That person may come to assist you to the next level, and when his or her time is up, you must be okay with it. Do not try to hold on to people when their time is up. It is always

Everyone who comes into your life is not there for a lifetime.

STEWARDSHIP

wise that when someone comes into your life, you ask God who it is and why he or she is there.

Psalm 1:1 says, "Blessed is the man that walketh not in the counsel of the ungodly, nor standeth in the way of sinners, nor sitteth in the seat of the scornful. But his delight is in the law of the Lord." We ought to be careful where we take our counsel/advice from. If our counselor/advisor is not born of God, then we will be walking in error. In other words, as a child of God, you cannot go to a psychic or tarot reader for instructions for your godly path. We must establish good, healthy relationships.

> *We must establish good, healthy relationships.*

In 1 Peter 3:1 it says, "Likewise, ye wives, be in subjection to your own husbands." Colossians 3:18 says, "Wives, submit yourselves unto your own husbands, as it is fit in the Lord." Ephesians 5:22-23 says, "Wives, submit yourselves unto your own husbands, as unto the Lord. For the husband is the head of the wife, even as Christ is the head of the church: and he is the savior of the body."

We live in a time where every aspect of life is so advanced, as opposed to the days of the Early Church. But what we must realize is that time and seasons may change, but the Word of God does not, and neither does God. Yesterday, today, and forever, He will be the same God. Amen! As women, our duty is to live in obedience to the Word of God because at the end of our lives (here on earth), we will give an account to God for how we lived this marriage relationship. Marriage was ordained by God, not man, and we do not want to be the one guilty of messing it up. When a wife rebels against her husband, she is in fact rebelling against God Himself. The times we are living in have changed. Women can do almost any job that men can, and there are no restrictions against that. There are many women whose income is much more than their husbands, but that does not mean that we get to rule over them. God Himself has positioned man, and we must respect God's authority because at the end of the day, man must answer to God. Haven't you noticed? No one lives forever. The reality is that when life comes to an end, we all must stand before God, and while some will meet Him as Savior, others will meet Him as Judge. We make our pick according to how we live our lives.

> *We make our pick according to how we live our lives.*

Take a look at this with me. Proverbs 18:22 says, "Whoso findeth a wife findeth a good thing, and obtaineth favour of the Lord." In the light of this verse, we must understand that the way God planned it is that a man should search for his wife. It is not a woman's duty to search for a husband. We are looking at a man who pursues a woman because he sees her as the person that he desires to spend the rest of his life with. Despite her much resistance, he pursues with all his might, bringing gifts and flowers. After a time, the woman gives in and decides to open her heart. This man takes her on dates to the finest restaurants. He makes her all kinds of promises, showing her what life will be like if she will accept him as her husband. Of course, the woman is going to fall for it because every woman is in search of love and security because that is how God made women. Every woman wants to be loved, and when she is loved, she loves back in return.

Now that the man has won her heart and she has accepted to be his wife, she is expecting that all those promises, gifts, flowers, and date nights will continue after the vows. Do you blame her for her expectations? You showed her what you were capable of, and she entered matrimony with expectancy. Now that you have her where you wanted her, in a matter of months, all the good times have ended, and there is no view of any promise you made her coming to pass. As a matter of fact, that wonderful man has stopped bringing flowers, there is no more time for date nights, and he seldom makes the time for a good conversation. This lady is now wondering who this man is and what happened to the man she dated who made her feel like a queen. She then begins to see that man as one who deceived and entrapped her. These practices should not be in the body of Christ.

It is not my intention to take sides. I am married to a wonderful man of God; I did not say perfect. I realize that when

Social

two persons in Christ come together, they both must have a word of confirmation from God before they join in matrimony. In my opinion, I do not think there are any "perfect marriages" because it is two different human beings with two different brains coming together in union. However, there are countless successful marriages! When you have a word from God, it's like security, no matter what mountain you arrive at or what valley you encounter. And because you got a word from God before you entered the union, you can always go back to God and say, "Father, You gave me this word. You endorsed this, so show us the way." When two persons come together with an endorsement from God, there is a wonderful spirit of understanding that resides with them. Understanding is key!

Understanding is key!

My advice to anyone who wants to get married is seek God for a word of confirmation concerning that person you are looking at or who has approached you. Do not go into any relationship because of a physical attraction. Go into prayer and fasting and ask God for confirmation. He will give you a word as He has given many of us in the past. There are too many divorces today.

In biblical days, women stayed home and took care of the home and family while men went out to work. The men were the sole breadwinners. It is not so today. Life is a hustle, and living is expensive, so the world is divided into classes—the rich, the upper class, the lower class, and the poor. There is a financial struggle in possibly 50 percent of every home or more, and because of this, both parents must go out to work in order to make ends meet. Women go for the highest education just as men, and in many cases, we have women who make much more money than their husbands. But the Word of God has not and will not change. Wives are to submit to and revere their husbands (Eph. 5:33).

It does not matter what status you have attained in this world or if your income is twice that of your husband. Wives, we must honor the Word of God in our lives. If we do not, it means we are living in rebellion against God. What does the Bible say about rebellion?

Husbands, the Bible commands you to love your wives, to love them as you love your own bodies. Ephesians 5:25 says, "Husbands, love your wives, even as Christ also loved the church, and gave himself for it." Verses 28-29 say, "So ought men to love their wives as their own bodies. He that loveth his wife loveth himself. For no man ever yet hated his own flesh, but nourisheth and cherisheth it, even as the Lord the church." Verse 31 says, "For this cause shall a man leave his father and mother, and shall be joined unto his wife, and they two shall be one flesh." Colossians 3:19 says, "Husbands, love your wives, and be not bitter against them."

Social

In the above quoted scriptures, the Bible shows that the duty of love has been imposed on the man. Why? Because God took a rib out of man and made woman. Woman was made from man. When a man takes a wife, it is as if he has taken his rib, so his responsibility is to love and cherish her and treat her as his very flesh. Thus, God gave man the command to love the woman, and the woman is commanded to submit to him. When a man takes a wife and does it the biblical way, it goes as God has planned. You may ask, how is that possible?

In 1 Peter 3:7 (AMP) it says, "Husband ought to live with their wives in an understanding manner (with great gentleness and tact and with an intelligent regard for the marriage relationship), so that your prayer will not be hindered or ineffective." The key words in that verse are understanding, gentleness, tact, and intelligent regard for the marriage relationship. Therefore, husbands, if you are experiencing problems in your marriage, just pause and ask yourself these questions: "Am I operating in the spirit of understanding? Am I operating in the spirit of gentleness (which is part of God's character)? Am I tactful in my dealings with issues? In all that I do, am I demonstrating an intelligent regard for the marriage relationship?" If your answer is no, then look at the end of the verse: "So that your prayer will not be hindered nor ineffective." If you do not live your marriage the biblical way, husbands, God will not hear your prayers. God has no intentions of adjusting His Word for you and me. His Word is His bond. Marriage ought not to be taken lightly, and when a man takes a woman to be his wife, it is a profoundly serious matter before God.

Ephesians 6:1 and Colossians 3:20: "This is a charge to children that children ought to be obedient to parents."

Ephesians 6:3 says, "That in so doing it will be well with you children and your days on earth will be prolonged." This means that children who are disobedient to parents will have their days shortened on earth.

At the same time, Ephesians 6:4 says, "That fathers should not provoke their children to wrath." Do not give them an occasion to be in rebellion against you but bring them up in the nurture and admonition of the Lord.

Proverbs 17:17 says, "A friend loveth at all times." True friends will stick with you in good times and in bad. You do not need to hang on to those who walk away from you when you are at your lowest. Just let them go.

Invest in your relationships—marriage, family, friendships. Husbands and wives, it is important to have a night set aside each week just for the two of you (your date night). It is also important to have a time of devotion, just the two of you spending time together in the Word of God and prayer, praying for each other's needs and against anything that is not of God. It's important to establish a day of fasting to kill your flesh and strengthen your spirit. We must remember that the enemy's intention is to destroy marriage because it is God-ordained. We can't afford to give him any place in our marriages. Develop clear lines of communication. Be each other's best friend. Listen to each other. Do not look outside for people to confide in but be each other's confidant. Encourage and strengthen one another. Be each other's biggest fan because in so doing, you establish trust, which is a major necessity in marriage.

What is going on in your marriage right now? Do you still love, honor, and respect each other? Is there free communication between you and your spouse? Can you have a conversation without fighting/quarrelling? Are you each other's best friend, or do you seek solace elsewhere? Do you pray and fast together? Do you spend quality time together, like setting aside a specific evening for a date night or just quality time for good conversation? What is the relationship between you and your children? Can they freely and comfortably converse with you, or do you get to know about them through someone else? What kind of friends do you keep? Are they assets to your Christian life, or do they fall in the bracket of liabilities? If your friends are important to you, how do you relate to/treat them? What is your relationship with your parents—do you honor them?

LET US PRAY:

Heavenly Father, I thank you for Your Word. I repent for the relationships in my life that I have been taking for granted. I repent for the relationships that I have destroyed through ignorance. Lord, I ask You to forgive me for all those who I have wounded and/or offended, whether consciously or unconsciously. I receive Your forgiveness, in Jesus's name. Lord, help me to be a better friend to those in and out of the body of Christ and my family. Help me to demonstrate patience, kindness, and mercy to those who need it, recognizing my own imperfections. Help me to be a friend who will always love, even when it is difficult to do so. Help me to forgive, be patient, and be longsuffering where I need to. Lord, considering Your Word, I examine my actions in my marriage. I understand that I and my mate are one.

Today, I commit myself to walk in agreement with my mate, honoring Your Word and knowing that You ordained marriage to show forth Your love for the church. Every door that we have opened and allowed the enemy to come in and put a wedge between us, we repent of. On the authority of Your Word, Lord, we bind and cast out every spirit that we have allowed in, and we command them to catch fire right now, in Jesus's name. We shut every door that we have opened, and we call on the Holy Spirit to saturate our lives and our home. Help us as a couple to walk in the Spirit and allow our lives to be led by Your Spirit, Lord. Lord, help us to love, honor, and respect one another even as Christ loves the church. Bind us together, Lord, with Your cords of love that cannot be broken. Heal our hearts from the pains of deception, disappointment, and despair, oh, Lord.

I no longer want to continue living in rebellion, Lord. I repent for everywhere that my actions and attitude were contrary to Your Word and caused unnecessary pain and stress to my mate. Lord, help me to foster good and healthy relationships, in Jesus's name. Amen.

Financial

I grew up with a father who taught my siblings and I how to protect ourselves financially. He demonstrated to us how to work hard and always to put something aside for rainy days. That means that on a day when you have nowhere to reap, you can go into your storehouse. He taught us how to invest in savings so that we would never be borrowers but always able to lend. He taught us that if we manage our resources well, we will never have to be jealous of anyone but will be able to buy whatever we need in life. My father's principles were adapted from the Word of God, but I never realized that until I came into the body of Christ. As I walk through life, I have found this sound advice which is based on the Word of God to really be an asset to me financially.

Proverbs 21:20: "There is treasure to be desired and oil in the dwelling of the Wise; but a foolish man spendeth it up."

Proverbs 13:16: "Every prudent man dealeth with knowledge: but a fool layeth open his folly."

STEWARDSHIP

Luke 14:28-30 "For which of you, intending to build a tower, sitteth not down first, and counteth the cost, whether he have sufficient to finish it?

Lest haply, after he hath laid the foundation, and is not able to finish it, all that behold it begin to mock him,

Saying, This man began to build, and was not able to finish."

Proverbs 6:6-8: "Go to the ant, you sluggard; consider its ways and be wise! It has no commander, no overseer or ruler, yet it stores provisions in summer and gathers its food at harvest."

1 Corinthians 16:2: "On the first day of every week, each one of you should set aside a sum of money in keeping with your income, saving it up, so that when I come no collections will have to be made."

Proverbs 27:12: "The prudent see danger and take refuge, but the simple keep going and pay the penalty."

Proverbs 30:24-25: "Four things on earth are small yet are extremely wise. Ants are creatures of little strength, yet they store up their food in the summer."

Ecclesiastes 11:2: "Invest in seven ventures, yes in eight; you do not know what disaster may come upon the land."

Financial

Proverbs 13:11: "Dishonest money dwindles away, but he who gathers money little by little makes it grow."

Proverbs 28:20: "A faithful man will abound with blessings, but he who makes haste to be rich will not be unpunished."

Ecclesiastes 7:12: "For wisdom is a defense and money is a defense."

Ecclesiastes 10:19: "But money answereth all things."

As children of God, we cannot be unwise—not in this season. We cannot continue to live from paycheck to paycheck. We must seek God for the wisdom of stewardship where our finances are concerned.

God has given us the formula in His Word. In Proverbs 6:6-8, He said: "Look at the ant. Such a small creature. Almost microscopic. Look at their lifestyle and gain wisdom from it. The ants have no commander, no overseer or ruler, yet they store their provisions in Summer. Summer is the productive season. Almost everything brings forth fruit in the Summer and after Summer, its Fall which is followed by Winter."

After summer, there are two changes of seasons. In these two seasons, no trees produce fruit, at least not here in the United States where we experience snowy weather. You

STEWARDSHIP

must wait for another season of spring and summer. The ant is wise enough with no ruler nor commander-in-chief to store up for the seasons when there is no produce.

God is saying to His children to follow the example of this extremely small creature. Do not waste all your resources at once. Store up for a season when you or your spouse may be out of a job, have a medical condition, or may be just in a financial bind. No matter how small you may think your income is, always put a fraction of it aside as savings. Over time, it builds up and brings a smile to your face and peace to your heart. When you go shopping, concentrate on that which you need and not that which you want because someone else has it. Stop wasting your food, water, clothing, etc. Always remember that there are less fortunate people who would wake up and be happy to have what you have thrown into your garbage.

We can apply the same principle to the Word. We must feed our spirit man now. We must do like David and hide the Word of God in our hearts because we do not know when there will arise a famine for the Word of God.

The Bible says in Ecclesiastes 11:2 (NIV) that "we should invest in seven ventures, yes, in eight. You do not know what disaster may

> *He wants us to have multiple streams of income so that we will have a financial advantage here on earth.*

Financial

come upon the land." God does not want us to just have savings but to invest in different ventures. He wants us to have multiple streams of income so that we will have a financial advantage here on earth.

Stewardship in the form of wise investing can be immensely helpful. When we make wise investments, we expose ourselves to a life of financial freedom.

Stewardship in the form of wise investing can be immensely helpful. When we make wise investments, we expose ourselves to a life of financial freedom.

God has given us the formula for our prosperity, but we are seated while the wicked man has picked up the formula our Father has given us. He is applying that formula and getting wealthier and wealthier while we sit back and look at him. We need to move into the kingdom mindset and apply all that the Word says about us.

A few years ago, I worked on this job where I got a good salary. After a period, I was given a raise, and I decided that I would pay my tithe out of that raise and put the balance away. I used an empty juice carton with the twist cap on the side to make it difficult to access. I did that for about eight months, and I arrived at a place where I needed to make a very important purchase, so I opened the carton to discover that I had saved over $2,000. I did this to prove to myself that I didn't need to live above my means because I realized that the practice of the more money you earn, the more you spend really doesn't have to be.

Luke 6:38 says, "Give, and it shall be given unto you; good measure, pressed down, and shaken together, and running over, shall men give into your bosom. For with the same measure that ye mete withal it shall be measure to you again." 2 Corinthians 8:1-5 says, "The churches of Macedonia giving out of lack..." Acts 4:32 says, "The people shared what they had with one another, they called nothing their own" (MSG). Malachi 3:10 says, "Bring all the tithes into the storehouse" (MSG). I remember when I moved from one state and I was searching for a church to settle in. I made sure that I took my tithes out of every week's pay and put them away until I found a ministry to settle and sow into. It is so important not to touch that which belongs to the Lord.

Another principle that I applied to my life and still do today is giving God my first fruit. At the beginning of every year, I ensure that I give half of my first salary to God. I have been doing that for many years, and I seal it with the prayer, "Lord, let me never be without a job, and let me have the privilege of choosing how long I want to stay home between jobs," and God has always honored my faith. I always remind myself that it is God who has given me the health and strength to work and that I am just a steward over the

Financial

paycheck I receive. Therefore, I always seek to be a blessing to someone and never hold money with a tight fist.

Giving is one of the Bible's principles to improve one's life financially. Sadly, we see the people of the world embracing this principle, and they are increasing tremendously. Look at the movie stars, the sports stars, and the celebrities. When you listen to them, they have some foundation, community, school, or organization in which they sow large sums of money. This biblical principle works for them because it is available to all those who will apply it.

> *Giving is one of the Bible's principles to improve one's life financially.*

Child of God, why don't you sow also so that you can reap a good measure that is pressed down and running over? Malachi 3:8 and 10 say:

> Will a man rob God? yet ye have robbed me. But ye say, wherein have we robbed thee? In tithes and offerings. Bring ye all the tithes into the storehouse, that there may be meat in mine house, and prove me now herewith, saith the Lord of hosts, if I will not open you the windows of heaven, and pour you out a blessing, that there shall not be room enough to receive it.

STEWARDSHIP

To withhold one's tithes is to commit an offense directly against God.

Whatever finance comes into our hands, we must give God a tithe from it. Giving your tithes is opening your life to increase and abundance. Withholding your tithes is shutting your doors to prosperity and abundance. A tithe is one-tenth, in case you are not aware, and when you withhold your tithes from God, you are setting yourself up for hardship and poverty. A tithe is not only required from the saints but from every apostle, prophet, bishop, evangelist, missionary, pastor, etc. Everyone in the body of Christ, whether you are a leader or just a follower, is required to give back to God one tenth of that which He has allowed to come into your hand. Do not rob God. It is a sin, and no sin can enter heaven.

When you align yourself with the Word of God, in a time of drought, you can freely petition God, and He will show up on your behalf because His Word is His bond. He is a God who cannot lie. When you do not align yourself with the Word of God, in a time of drought, you will suffer.

Financial

When you give and pay your tithes, it is like going into the bank and opening a savings account and constantly adding more and more to it. When you arrive at a place of need in your life, you can go to the bank and make withdrawals because you it belongs to you. But if you try to go to the bank and withdraw money that you did not save, you could be arrested and jailed for fraud. God is against every evil means that we would seek to engage in in order to prosper. That is why He gave us a simple formula—**give and pay your tithes.** Stop living from paycheck to paycheck. Stop going after wants and focus on needs.

> *Everyone in the body of Christ, whether you are a leader or just a follower, is required to give back to God one tenth of that which He has allowed to come into your hand. Do not rob God. It is a sin, and no sin can enter heaven.*

God wants us to be free to spread the good news of the kingdom, but how can we fulfill the Great Commission of Matthew 28:19 if we are bound by jobs as slaves? It is time for the church to be rid of all selfishness of the flesh and live as a community. God has given us talents and skills that we can use to employ ourselves. What is it that you are good at? Ask yourself this question. Then see how you can find a way to invest that talent. Become self-employed and employ others in the kingdom so that you and I can be free to fulfill the Great Commission.

STEWARDSHIP

We must be careful, though, because many in the kingdom can't manage prosperity. As soon as their pockets are full, they forget God and become independent. Others become greedier and greedier and do not follow what the Word says in Matthew 6:19, "Lay not up for yourselves treasures on earth, where moth and rust doth corrupt, and where thieves break through and steal."

God wants us to be a success, but our success must be in direct accordance with His Word. We must seek the kingdom first. According to Matthew 6:33, "But seek ye first the kingdom of God, and his righteousness; and all these things shall be added unto you." Luke 12:31 says, "God wants us to be dependent on Him." He wants our total lives on earth to glorify Him. If you live a life independent of God, you are not bringing glory to Him.

Proverbs 3:5-6 says, "Trust in the Lord with all thine heart." Hebrews 10:38 says, "The just shall live by faith." We must be totally and constantly dependent upon God. He wants to always be the supplier of our needs.

Deuteronomy 8:18: "But thou shalt remember the Lord thy God: For it is he that giveth thee power to get wealth that he may establish covenant."

The power to get wealth belongs to God.

Financial

Budgeting is an important part of managing your resources because it enables you to give confidently instead of simply wondering if you can contribute.

1. Give tithes and offerings.

2. Take care of bills.

3. Pay yourself.

4. Put money toward your savings.

5. Put money toward an emergency fund.

6. Sow a seed into someone's life.

> *Budgeting is an important part of managing your resources*

What kind of income do you have? Where do you observe immediate leakage in your finances? What plans do you have for your future? Do you have a financial plan? Have you ever met with a financial planner? What adjustments are you willing to make to attain your financial goals? Are you a tither? Are you a giver?

LET US PRAY:

Lord, I come to You today and first repent for my lack of proper stewardship of the finances that You have given me. I thank you for allowing me to understand that it is You who have given me the ability to gain wealth and that it is You who have given me health and strength. Without you, I would not even be able to hold a job.

I'm asking for Your wisdom in the management of my finances. Lord, I have been operating in ignorance, but I thank you for the light that Your Word has shone upon me. Father, I ask You to first touch my mind as I have not been thinking in accordance to the kingdom. I pray for a redirection of my mind. I bind every spirit that has been an influence on my financial discomfort, and I shut down their enterprises, in Jesus's name. I bind lack, poverty, stinginess, selfishness, and every other spirit unleashed against me to block me from prospering financially. Help me, Lord, to live within my means and not above. Help me to attend to my needs and not my wants.

Lord, I thank you for that skill You have given me/that business idea (**name it**). I thank you for opening doors of opportunity for me. I call into divine alignment all those You have ordained to assist me to my financial destination. I thank you for delivering me from the spirit of fear and everything that has held me back from entering my purpose, Lord. Help me, Lord, to be wiser in all my financial dealings. From today onward, I declare You Lord over my finances, and I thank you for Your divine intervention and direction, in Jesus's name.

Financial

I seal up every area of leakage in my spiritual, mental, physical, social, and financial lives with the blood of Jesus. Devil, you have stolen enough, and you shall steal no more. I command the restoration of all the years that the locust and the cankerworm have eaten in the time of my ignorance.

I decree and declare that I have the victory! I'm an overcomer and no longer walking in darkness, but I am risen to a new life, and by God's power, I will live. Amen.

Citations:

Page 1: Definition of Stewardship- Wikipedia

https://en.wikipedia.org/wiki/Stewardship

- This page was last edited on 13 August 2020, at 07:12 (UTC).
- Text is available under the Creative Commons Attribution-ShareAlike License; additional terms may apply. By using this site, you agree to the Terms of Use and Privacy Policy. Wikipedia® is a registered trademark of the Wikimedia Foundation, Inc., a non-profit organization.
- Privacy policy
- About Wikipedia

Page 5: definition of Preserved

Webster's 1828 Dictionary.com

STEWARDSHIP

Page 10

Got questions.org

The 8 different types of prayers mentioned:

The prayer of Faith, The prayer Agreement, the prayer of Request, The prayer of thanksgiving,

The prayer of Worship, The prayer of Consecration, The prayer of Intercession and the prayer od Imprecation,

© Copyright 2002-2020 Got Questions Ministries. All rights reserved. Privacy Policy

This page last updated: January 2, 2020

Page 17

Sleep has great benefits, it's a natural healer.

From:VeryWellHealth.com

Verywellhealth.com

Top of Form

Daily Health Tips to Your Inbox

Citations:

SIGN UP

Bottom of Form

Follow Us<u>Privacy Policy</u>

Visit our other Verywell sites:

Verywell FitVerywell MindVerywell Family

(IMAGE 1 HERE)

© 2020 About, Inc. (Dotdash) — All rights reserved

Page 19

The meaning of "sacrifice" Merriam Webster's dictionary

Page 19 – according to Merriam Webster's dictionary the word "Immoral" means

Page 25- according to Merriam Webster's dictionary the word "hostile" means:

© 2020 Merriam-Webster, Incorporated

Page 20

According to vocabulary.com, "chastisement" means: Policy.

COPYRIGHT NOTICE: Copyright ©2020 Thinkmap, Inc., 599 Broadway, 9th Floor, New York, New York 10012. All rights reserved.

TRADEMARKS. Plumb Design, Thinkmap, vocabulary.com, VQ, Informotion, and Visual Thesaurus are either trademarks or registered trademarks of Thinkmap, Inc. or its affiliates or licensors. The names of other companies and products mentioned on or via the Site may be the trademarks of their respective owners. Reference to such third party trademarks is for informational purposes only and is not intended to indicate or imply any affiliation, association, sponsorship, or endorsement. Any rights not expressly granted herein are reserved.

13. Content Specific Notices: Some of the definitions that appear on the site are from WordNet:

WordNet License

WordNet 3.0 Copyright 2006 by Princeton University. All rights reserved. THIS SOFTWARE AND DATABASE IS PROVIDED "AS IS" AND PRINCETON UNIVERSITY MAKES NO REPRESENTATIONS OR WARRANTIES,

Citations:

EXPRESS OR IMPLIED. BY WAY OF EXAMPLE, BUT NOT LIMITATION, PRINCETON UNIVERSITY MAKES NO REPRESENTATIONS OR WARRANTIES OF MERCHANT- ABILITY OR FITNESS FOR ANY PARTICULAR PURPOSE OR THAT THE USE OF THE LICENSED SOFTWARE, DATABASE OR DOCUMENTATION WILL NOT INFRINGE ANY THIRD PARTY PATENTS, COPYRIGHTS, TRADEMARKS OR OTHER RIGHTS. The name of Princeton University or Princeton may not be used in advertising or publicity pertaining to distribution of the software and/or database. Title to copyright in this software, database and any associated documentation shall at all times remain with Princeton University and LICENSEE agrees to preserve same.

Page: 22

Buddha Quotes. 'the mind is a powerful thing to waste" Which is a form of the Slogan "A mind is a terrible thing to waste" coined by Arthur fletcher of the United Negro College fund. 1972.

General Citation: all scripture quotations are taken from the King James Version of the Bible.

CPSIA information can be obtained
at www.ICGtesting.com
Printed in the USA
LVHW051620120221
679183LV00009B/820